← Use pencils so you can draw lightly at first, and then go over the lines you like.

← artist-type hat

Don't use paints or the paper will wrinkle up — remember, I warned you!

Crayons and colored pencils are good, too.
←

Amelia's Easy-as-Pie Drawing Guide

by Marissa Moss

(and quick-on-the-draw Amelia!)

How to draw a pie:

① Make a circle.

② Add a wavy line all around for the crust.

③ Put four dark teardrops in the middle so it doesn't look like a fried egg.

④ Cut yourself a slice and eat!

Can I have some pie?

American Girl®

← I like markers, but they may show through on the other side of the page.

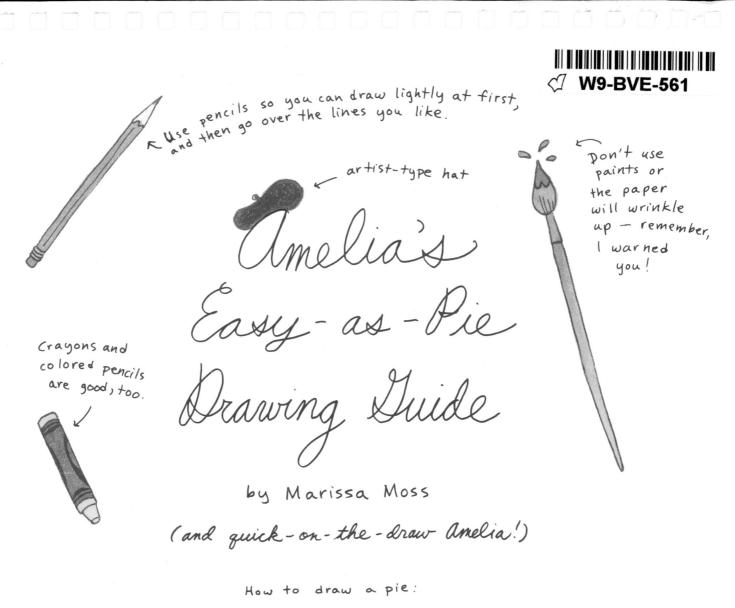

Here it is — y<u>our</u> sketchbook! Aren't your fingers just itching to put marks on all these blank pages? Don't worry about making mistakes — some of my best drawings came from mistakes. (I just had to figure out how to use them.)

The way you draw is like the way you speak — everyone sounds and draws their own way. I don't care if I can draw something EXACTLY the way it looks, but I want it to look like <u>I</u> drew it. That's Amelia style!

Some people draw with **STRONG** lines. ↓

Some people draw with wispy lines. ↓

Some people don't like to use outlines at all. ↓

I don't have enough patience to draw like this. ↗

Draw whatever way feels best to y<u>ou</u>!

I <u>LOVE</u> to draw, and I've been drawing ever since I could hold a crayon  (I think I was two). I draw on my tests, on homework, even on the bottom of my bed (my mom wasn't too happy about <u>that</u> when she found out).

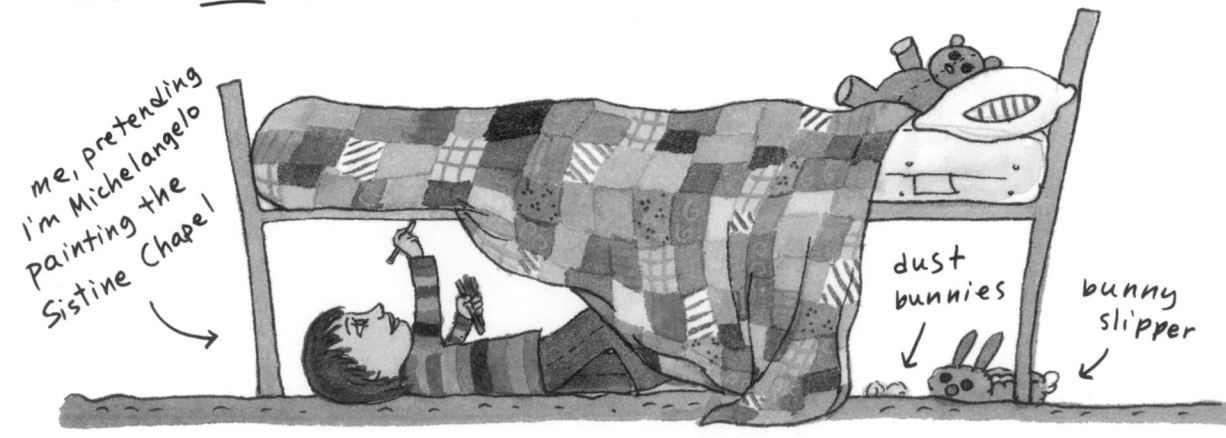

me, pretending I'm Michelangelo painting the Sistine Chapel ↘

dust bunnies ↓

bunny slipper ↙

So I would say the best way to learn to draw is do it, do it, DO IT! The more you draw, the better you'll get.

How do you draw a dog? How do you draw a person?
↓

Here's how I drew a dog when I was three.
↓

↑
looks like a balding sun — not a dog

when ↑ I was five

↑
when I was seven (looks like a sheep really)

↑
Here's how I draw a dog now!

Here's how I drew a person when I was three.
↘

↑
looks like a very bald sun

↑
when I was five (at least there's a body!)

↑
when I was seven (no more sticks!)

↑
How I draw now!

USE YOUR EYES!

Learning to draw is also learning to SEE. You have to
see something in your __head__ before you can draw it on paper.
One way to practice seeing (and drawing) is to look at
shapes and __see__ what they can be — then draw the rest.

Now y__ou__ try, with these shapes:
↓

↑
This
can be a
party
hat.
↓

or a
lion's nose
↓

or a
rhino's horn
↓

↑
Can't you <u>tell</u>
this is a rhino?

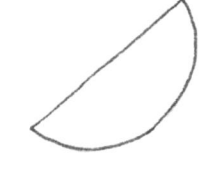

Here are some
hints if you're
stuck.
↓

↑
a ladybug

↑
a sinking boat

a ram's horn

Hey!
↑
a jelly-roll nose

What can you make out of these shapes?
↓

more
hints
↓

more
hints
↓

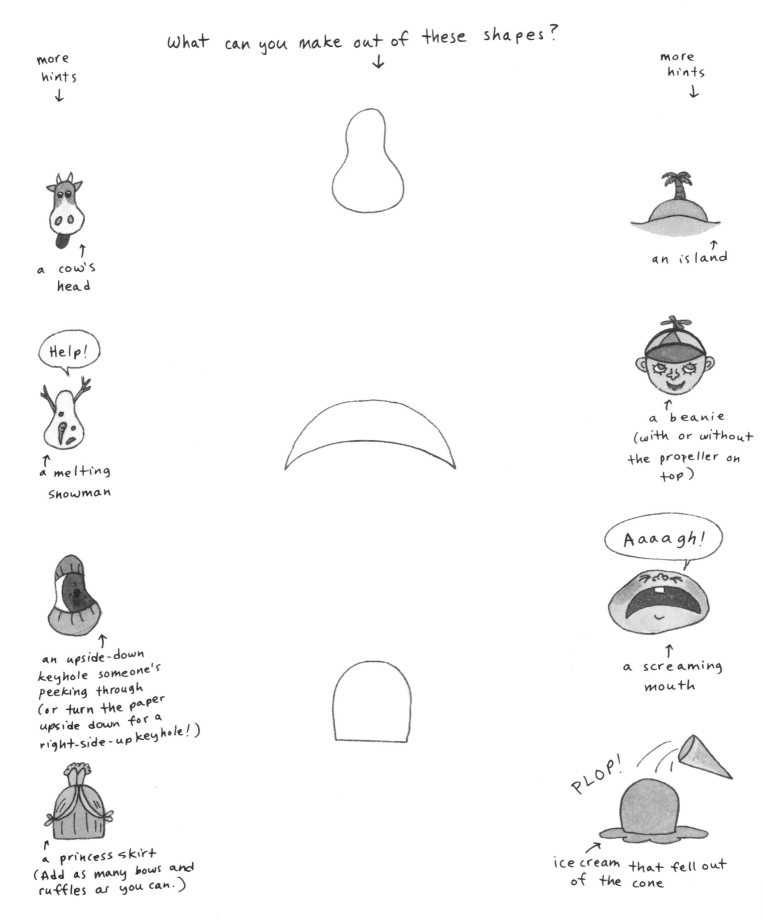

a cow's
head

an island

Help!

a beanie
(with or without
the propeller on
top)

a melting
snowman

Aaaagh!

an upside-down
keyhole someone's
peeking through
(or turn the paper
upside down for a
right-side-up keyhole!)

a screaming
mouth

PLOP!

a princess skirt
(Add as many bows and
ruffles as you can.)

ice cream that fell out
of the cone

WHAT'S MY LINE?

Sometimes when I don't know what to draw, I draw a line and then see what it turns into. That's another way of learning to see — and learning to draw!

What do you see in these lines?

an elephant's ear

a bird's wing

becomes a nose

a line

an ocean wave

an elf hat

a tree

becomes legs walking

a line

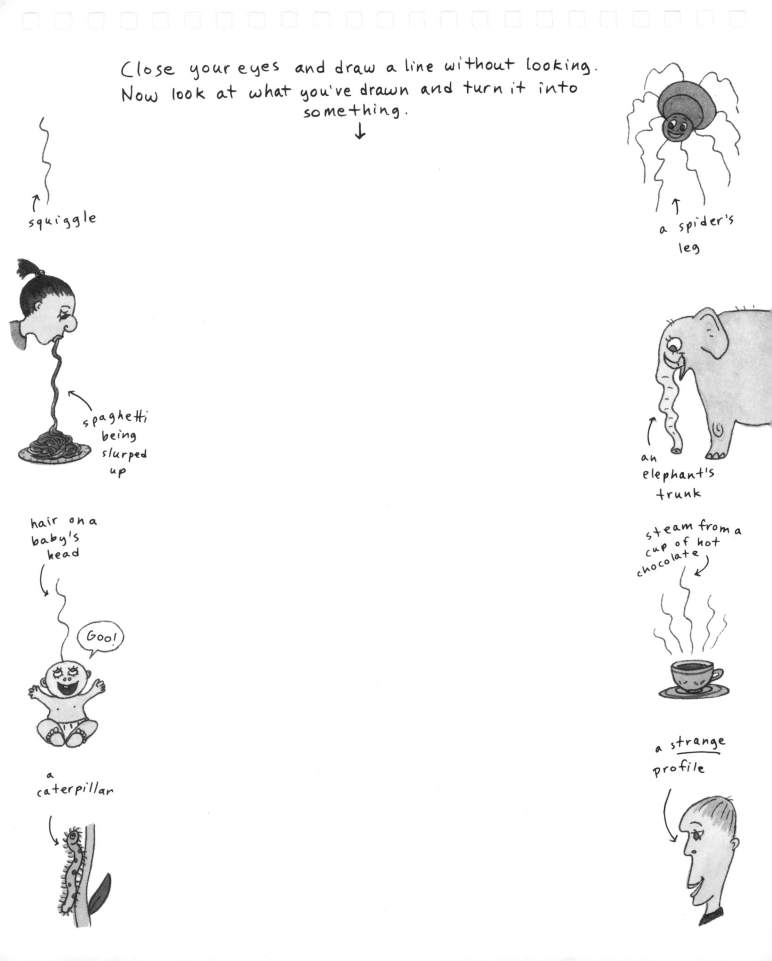

Close your eyes and draw a line without looking. Now look at what you've drawn and turn it into something.
↓

↑
squiggle

a spider's leg
↑

spaghetti being slurped up

an elephant's trunk

hair on a baby's head

Goo!

steam from a cup of hot chocolate

a caterpillar

a strange profile

L I N E  U P

clothesline ↗

A line can be just a line, but it can also be the edge of something. Or it can show you where the ground is so your drawings don't just float in space. Here are some lines for you to play with. Are they the ground or part of something?

↓

the ground ↑

a wall someone peeks over ↑

a mouse tail ↑

the edge of a book ↑
(or notebook!)

part of a ↗ present (for me?)

the horizon where the sun sets ↑

a railroad track ↑
(or a ladder on its side)

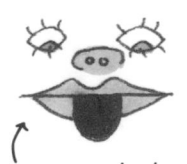

the line between two lips ↖

Here's another kind of line: Pick something you can look at to draw. (Shoes are very good for this.) Draw the outline of whatever it is in one line, <u>without</u> lifting up your pencil from the paper. Look <u>only</u> at the thing you're drawing, not at your paper.

↓

Here's what <u>my</u> drawings look like when I do this:

part of head here ↳

other part here ↙

↑ stuffed bunny

fork — <u>not</u> a hand ↓

scissors ↓

I added the drips afterward.

teapot ↗

It doesn't make a beautiful drawing, but it really makes you <u>look</u> at something. →

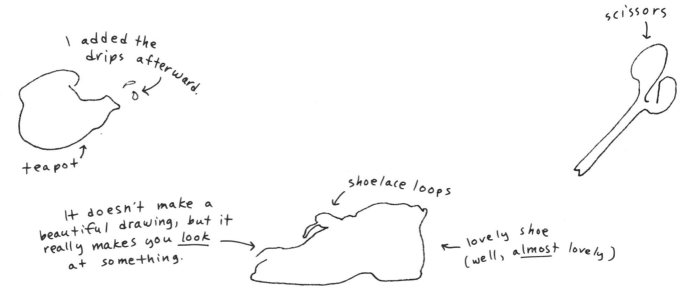

shoelace loops ↙

← lovely shoe (well, a<u>lmost</u> lovely)

One, two,
one, two!

These are some step-by-step drawings to get you into a drawing mood.

You draw here (see how much space I give you?).
↓

Oof!

Hey, don't step on me!
↓

step-by-step
↓

To make a simple sandwich:

①

A thin rectangle is the top slice of bread.

②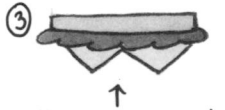

A ruffly shape will be the lettuce.

③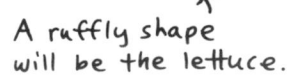

Triangles pointing down can be the cheese.

④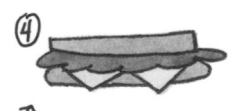

Curved lines like squashed balloons can be lunch meat, or — if you're a vegetarian — tomatoes.

⑤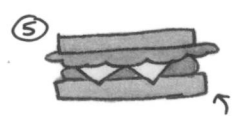

Now add the bottom slice of bread (another rectangle).

For a really big sandwich, repeat steps 1–5 over and over.
↓

If you get bored, add a fish here and there, or a drumstick, or even some eggs — anything you like!

Don't forget a squashed circle for the plate!

STEP-BY-STEP

You draw here.
↓

teacup
↓
① Draw a squashed oval.

② Draw a curved line under it.

③ Add a handle.

④ Put a bigger squashed oval underneath for a saucer.

⑤ Decorate however you like!

⑥ For more realism, add a curve of darker color inside the cup, and make wiggly lines above it for steam.

Band-Aid
↗
① Draw a square.

② Add rectangles with curved sides. (I know, then they're not rectangles, but you get the idea.)

③ Put small dots on the square part — TA DA!

pencil
↓
① Make a skinny rectangle with one ragged end.

② Put a triangle on the ragged part.

③ Add a curved rectangle with two lines in it on the other end.

④ Color it in and you're ready to draw! (A bite mark adds realism.)

STEP-BY-STEP BIRTHDAYS

Add a little rectangle to your balloon to make it look shiny!

Follow the steps here.
↓

If you curve two sides of the rectangle, it makes the balloon look rounder.

birthday cake
↓

① Start with a squashed oval.

② Add three sides of a curved rectangle under the oval.

③ Place a bigger squashed oval under it for a plate.

④ Now add fancy frosting.

⑤ Don't forget the candles!
(just skinny rectangles with teardrops on top)

Cut the cake!
↓

① Draw a squashed triangle like this.

② Put a rectangle under it.

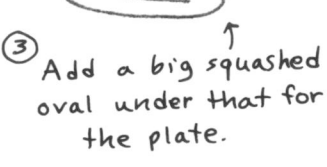

③ Add a big squashed oval under that for the plate.

④ Frosting time!

⑤ A candle makes it extra fancy.
(Now blow it out and make a wish!)

presents
↓

① Make any size rectangle.

② Put a bow on top.

③ Add a ribbon.

④ Decorate!

lotsa presents!

party hats
↓

① Start with a triangle that has a curved bottom.

② Top with a pompom...

... or a ribbon.

③ Decorate!

Let's have a party!

STEP ON IT!

You can use the step-by-step method to draw <u>anything</u>.
Just start with the biggest shapes and end with the details.
If something looks too complicated to draw, try making it
with your <u>own</u> step-by-step.

Your choice goes here.
↓

teddy
bear
↓

① Start with a
nice, round
number 8.

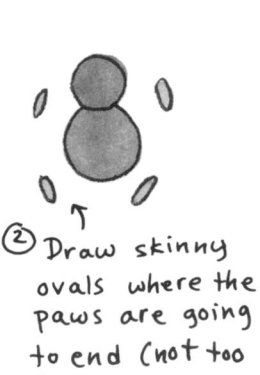

② Draw skinny
ovals where the
paws are going
to end (not too
far away or your
bear will have
skinny legs).

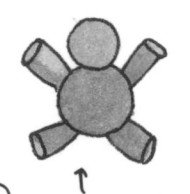

③ Connect the ovals to
the big circle with lines.

④ Finish with the details –
eyes, ears, nose, mouth,
and stitching!

frog
↓

① Start with
an 8 on its
side.

② Draw a
football under
the circles.

③ Make two curves
under the football.

④ Draw four lines
close together for
the front legs.

⑤ Add frog feet.

⑥ Don't forget
the face!

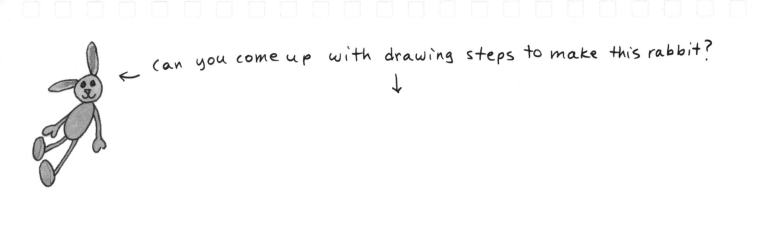
← Can you come up with drawing steps to make this rabbit?
↓

↑ How about a bunny slipper? ↘

← A teapot would be easy! →

← A shoe looks hard at first, but take it → apart step-by-step....
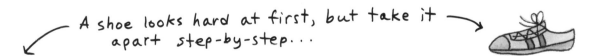

Here are the basic step-by-steps I use to draw dogs and cats. You can follow them or invent your own.

Your dog goes here.
↓

dog, side view
↓

① Make an oval for the body.

② Make a smaller oval above it and to the side for the head.

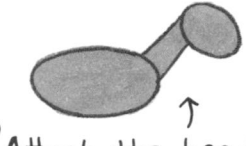

③ Attach the head to the body with two lines.

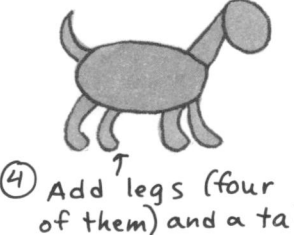

④ Add legs (four of them) and a tail.

⑤ Here's the tricky part — give your dog a face and ears. Add a tongue hanging out if you like.

dog, front view
↓

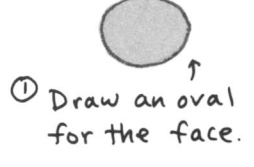

① Draw an oval for the face.

② Put a bigger oval under it like a squashed 8.

③ Add legs to the front and sides (like for your frog).

④ Draw a triangle flopped over a rectangle for each ear. Add a triangle tail.

⑤ Now give your pug a face!

cat lying down
↓

① Draw a circle with a bigger oval next to it.

② Add legs and a tail (one hind leg is hidden).

③ Add ears and make a face— don't forget whiskers!

cat standing up
↓

① Draw the circle and the oval again.

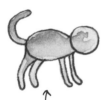

② This time the legs stand up, and the tail curls in.

③ Face time again!

Your cat goes here.
↓

cat sitting
↓

① Draw a circle on top of an oval.

② Draw the same kind of legs as for the dog's front view.

③ Curl the tail around and add triangle ears.

④ Give the cat a face.

⑤ For an even better cat, add stripes or other markings.

After you learn to draw a basic dog,
try drawing dogs with short legs, long legs,
curly tails, fluffy tails, poodle do's, and bows!
↓

You can do different
kinds of cats, too. Use shaggy
lines for thick fur or smooth
lines for
sleek fur.
↓

↑

For a kitten, make
the eyes rounder,
the tail shorter, and
the head bigger in
proportion to the
body.
↓

Pick an animal to draw.
↓

You can even turn your dog into a horse...
↓

← Add a mane and a long, curved neck.

Your cat can become a lion...
↓

Add a fluffy mane.

or a camel...
↓

← Add a hump, bumpy knees, cloven hooves, and a shaggy neck.

or a tiger...
↓

Add stripes and furry white cheeks.

... even a giraffe!
↓

← Add a really long neck, long legs, cloven hooves, horns, and splotches.

... even a catfish!
↓

(just kidding!)

For easy-as-pie faces, make a grid on a head to show you where to put the eyes, ears, nose, and mouth. After you've done it a few times, you won't need the grid.

Make a face!
↓

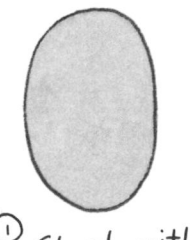

① Start with an oval.

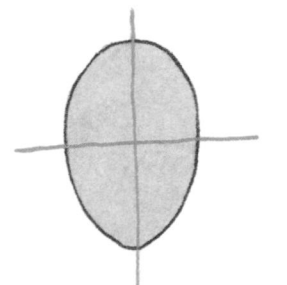

② Draw a horizontal line halfway up the oval, and another line right down the middle.

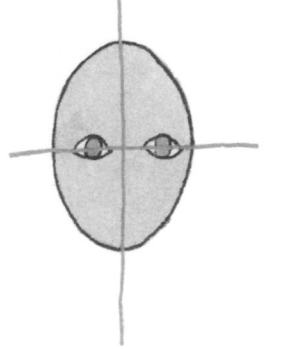

③ The eyes go on the horizontal line.

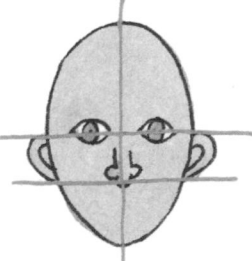

④ The bottoms of the nose and ears go halfway between the eyes and chin.

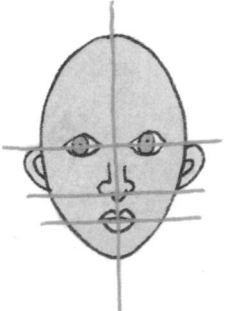

⑤ The mouth goes halfway between the nose and chin.

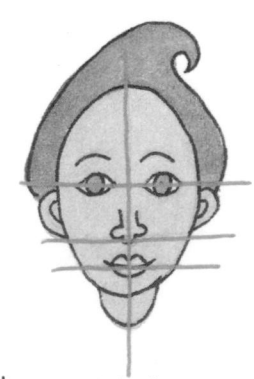

⑥ Now add hair, eyebrows, and a neck!

SIDE STEPS

The grid is the same for a side view of a head.

You try now!
↓

① Start with an oval.

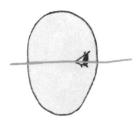

② Draw the eye halfway down. It looks like a sideways V.

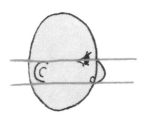

③ The bottoms of the nose and ear go halfway between the eye and chin.

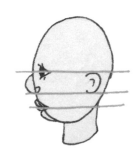

④ The mouth is halfway between the nose and chin. You can make it like a heart lying on its side.

⑤ Now add the neck and make the chin a little bigger.

⑥ Finish with the hair, eyebrow, and an earring if you want.

MAKE A FACE

Now that you know where things go, play around with different kinds of eyes, noses, and mouths.
↓

eyes
↓

happy eyes

mad eyes

scared eyes

suspicious eyes

tired eyes

alien eyes

bug eyes

loony eyes

mouths
↓

kissy lips

screaming mouth

laughing mouth

angry mouth

surprised mouth

chewing rudely mouth

noses
↓

button nose

U-turn nose

clover nose

holey nose

jelly-roll nose

sharp nose

elephant nose

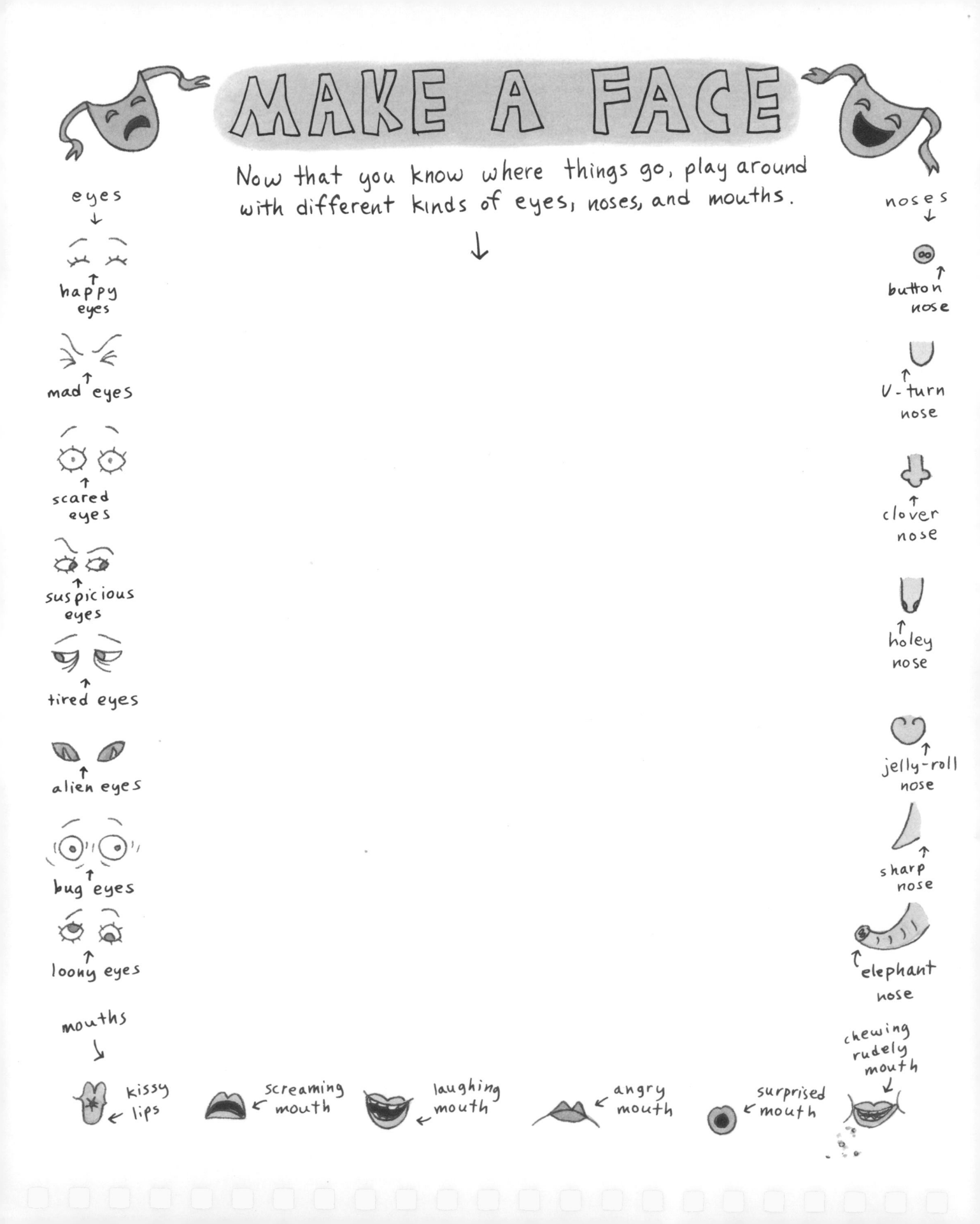

EXPRESS YOURSELF!

Eyes and mouths can show people's moods, but the trick to good expressions is eyebrows! Watch how this face changes when just the eyebrows move:

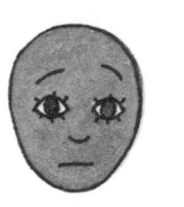 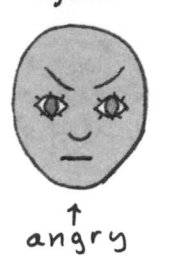 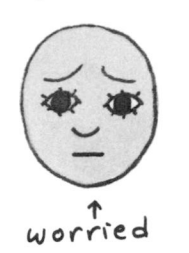 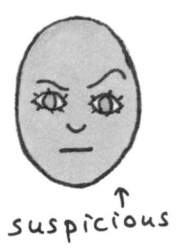

↑ concerned ↑ angry ↑ worried ↑ suspicious

Here's a place for <u>you</u> to play with eyebrows.

↓

If you change the mouth, too, you can do even more!

↓

happy ↑
(but bald)

↑ surprised to be bald

sad ↑ to still be bald

angry ↑
(Hey, what happened to my hair!)

↑ suspicious
(Did <u>you</u> take it?)

worried ↑
(Will I ever get it back?)

Make a face!

Add eyebrows to these faces.
↓

N<u>ot</u> the kind you make in a mirror.
<u>Draw</u> it!
↓

Add mouths to these.
↓

↑
You can add hair, too, if you want...

...or put hats on their heads.
↑

Amelia's Amazing Time Machine

↑ No messy machinery necessary!

Here's a simple trick to change the age of a face — the lower the eyes are on the head, the younger the person looks! How many different ages can you draw!

↑

↑ No assembly required!

↓ martian

↓ six-year-old

↑ baby

↓ regular person (someone my age, that is)

↑ one-year-old (less hair helps, too), as you get younger — and really old!)

↓ grown-up

two-year-old ↑

↑ old person (wrinkles add age)

PORTRAIT GALLERY

Now that you're an expert at faces, fill the picture frames with all kinds of people.

Frames are fun to draw, too!

↑ sleek, modern frame

↑ ornate gold frame

↑ joke frame made to look like a cow

↑ fancy frame with own light attached

↑ divided frame to hold lots of pictures at once

jewel-encrusted frame — must be someone very special!

HANDS-ON

Hands are the hardest. The trick is to always remember where to put the thumb.

① Start with a circle.

② Put the thumb down low.

③ Make sure you count the fingers as you draw them!

If your fingers are too fat, the hand will look like a flower.

If they're too thin, the hand will look like a fork.

Just right!

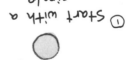

Now I'm handing this page over to you! ↑

left hand (Oops — it looks like a bunch of bananas!)

right hand (Oops — it's a claw!)

little bung too foo hand (first draw the thumb, then the two pointing fingers, then the two folded fingers.)

other hand making little bung too foo

fist (Draw the thumb first, then the fingers folded under it.)

other hand making a fist

If the position of the hand you're drawing is difficult, use your own hand as a model. It's usually best to draw the thumb first.

① To show a hand holding something, draw the thumb sticking out.

② Make the fingers like fat hot dogs lying next to the thumb. (Make sure they get smaller as you go toward the pinkie.)

↖ TA DA!

③ Add the thing being held.

↑
thumbs-up hand

↑
finger-pointing hand

↑
thumbs-down hand

↑
finger-walking hand

↑
O.K. hand

↑
clapping hands

↑
duck-quacking hand

↗
waiter hand

SOME BODY · ANY BODY

Sometimes it's easier to draw clothes than the body underneath.

① Start with the head and shirt.
② Add pants or a skirt.
③ Then draw hands and feet.

Hi there!

To put a person into a position is harder. For sitting, I draw the chair first, then fit the person into it.

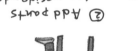

① Draw a sideways chair.
② Add pants (an upside-down L).
③ Draw the hand and arm.
④ Draw in the body.
⑤ Finish with the head and other arm and hand.

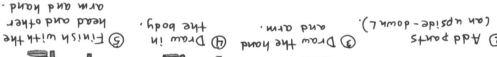

Here's room for your bodies. ↑

It's easier to draw if you go from part to part (like the step-by-steps) because you can't draw EVERYTHING at once — you'll just get frustrated. Start with whatever's easiest for you, then do the part that comes next, and keep going until you've drawn it all!

lying on your stomach
↓

① Start with a profile head.

② Drawing the ground can help you figure out where to put things, but draw the arm first.

③ Connect the head to the floor with the body.

④ Add legs — bend the knees, then finish with the feet.

Try an interesting body position (standing on your head, turning a cartwheel, diving, running, dancing, or jumping).
↓

To add spice to your people, give them personality! In fact, you can give <u>everything</u> you draw personality.

Don't just draw people like this.

Draw them like this!

snooty lady

artist

person having a bad-hair day

Goo!

cute little baby with very soggy diaper

Put some pizzazz in your pen!

Don't always draw chairs like this.

Draw some like these!

overstuffed armchair

swivelly office chair →

director's chair

country chair

royal chair (throne, that is)

baby's high chair

food smeared everywhere

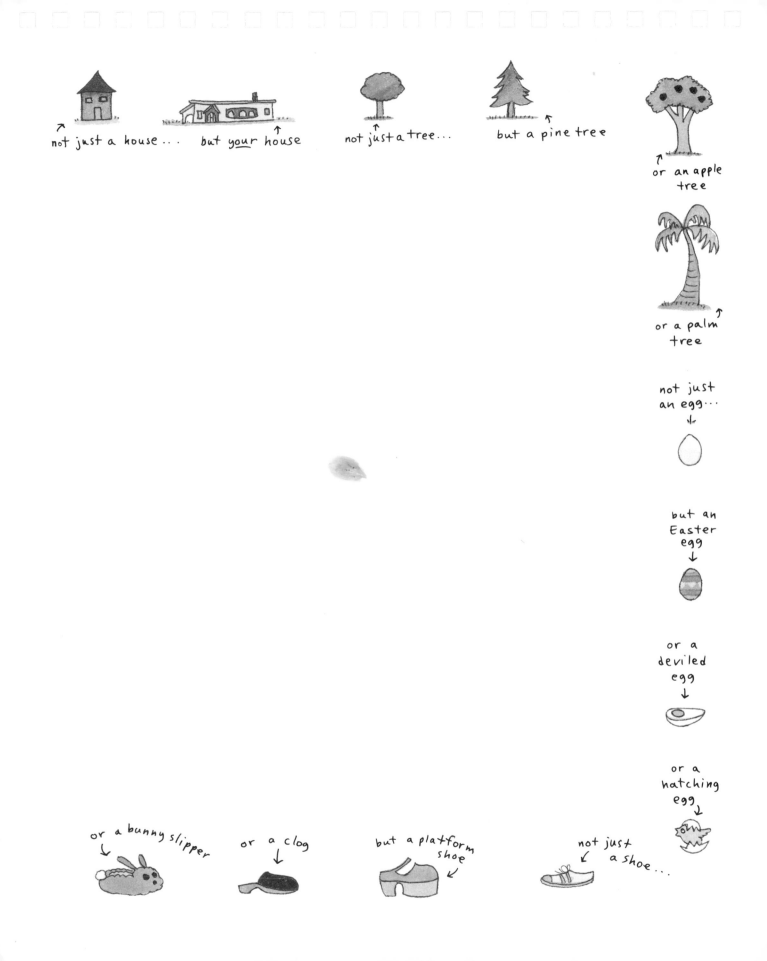

not just a house... but your house

not just a tree...

but a pine tree

or an apple tree

or a palm tree

not just an egg...

but an Easter egg

or a deviled egg

or a hatching egg

or a bunny slipper

or a clog

but a platform shoe

not just a shoe...

SHADOWS

Shadows are <u>so</u> cool! They're an easy, handy-dandy way to make anything look more real.

Wow!

Without a shadow, Cleo floats on air!

Hey!

Now she's firmly on the ground.

The trick with shadows is to make the outline match whatever is casting the shadow.

Purple works best for shadows. →

Looove my hair!

Me, too!

Draw the shadow for the lady and her poodle here. (This will be tricky, so be patient!)
↓

Now make drawings to go with the shadows.
↓

← an angel, please

← a horse, of course

Draw whatever you want <u>and</u> its shadow here.
↓

What's really cool is to make loooong shadows (then it seems later in the day because the sun is lower).
→

I've always wanted to be a giraffe!

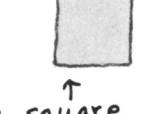 # PERSPECTIVE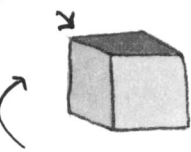

I'm not very good at this, but I still like to play with perspective—
it's a way of making things look 3-D. If you can make a 3-D box,
you can make almost anything!

 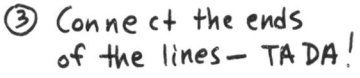

① Draw a square.

② Add diagonal lines coming off of three corners, all parallel to each other (like a table on its side).

③ Connect the ends of the lines— TA DA!

Make lots of boxes here.

↓

Boxes can turn into lots of other things.
Try it! (You can also start with a rectangle
in place of a square.)
↓

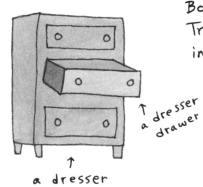

↑ a dresser
  drawer

↑
a dresser

↑
Change the
edges to make
a paper bag.

↑
Add a line
inside the box
and you can
put stuff in it!

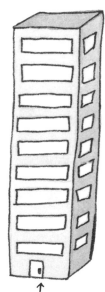

↑
Stretch the box
and you get a
skyscraper.

↑
A skinny box
can be a book —
or a notebook!

Add a roof for
a house (or a milk
carton).

↑
Add a
chimney (or a
straw).

Give it legs
and it's a
bathtub.

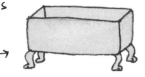

Add a face and a
body for a blockhead.

Add wheels and
the cab for a →
truck.

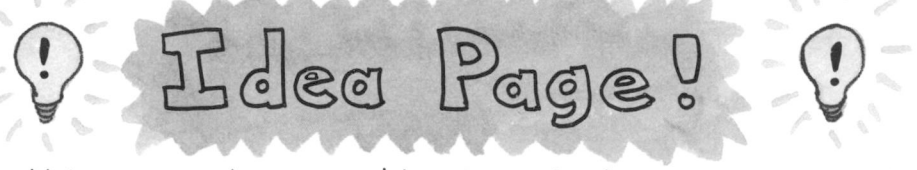

Idea Page!

Anything can give you ideas — just keep your eyes open. Draw what you ate for lunch, draw what you dreamed last night, or draw what you want to be when you grow up.
↓

Draw a monster.
↓

Draw a cookie and decorate it.
↓

Invent your own animal — part elephant, part bird, or part lion, part monkey.
↓

↑
This is a spotted implegoofus.

Draw a machine.
↓

↑
I don't know what it does, but it looks interesting.

CONGRATULATIONS

You're an artist now — draw yourself!

← Your name goes here.

← self-portrait of the artist — TA DA!

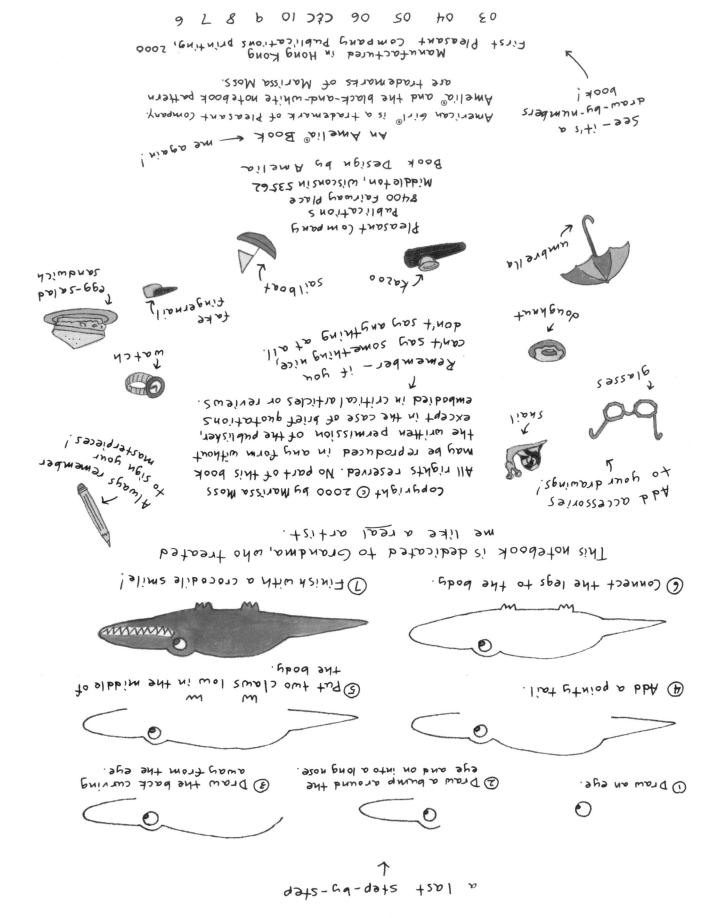

See - it's a draw-by-numbers book!

An Amelia® Book — me again!

Book Design by Amelia.

Pleasant Company
Publications
8400 Fairway Place
Middleton, Wisconsin 53562

sailboat

kazoo

umbrella

doughnut

egg-salad sandwich

fake fingernail

watch

Remember - if you can't say something nice, don't say anything at all.

glasses

snail

Add accessories to your drawings!

Always remember to sign your masterpieces!

This notebook is dedicated to Grandma, who treated me like a real artist.

① Draw an eye.

② Draw a bump around the eye and on into a long nose.

③ Draw the back curving away from the eye.

④ Add a pointy tail.

⑤ Put two claws low in the middle of the body.

⑥ Connect the legs to the body.

⑦ Finish with a crocodile smile!

a last step-by-step

Manufactured in Hong Kong
First Pleasant Company Publications printing, 2000

03 04 05 06 ??? 10 9 8 7 6